Chinese Running Script Calligraphy for Beginners

Wang Xianchun

Translated by Wen Jingen with Pauline Cherrett

CONFUCIUS INSTITUTE
at Colorado State University

FOREIGN LANGUAGES PRESS

Printed in China

中国国家汉办赠送
Donated by Hanban, China

First Edition 2007

Text by Wang Xianchun
English translation by Wen Jingen with Pauline Cherrett
Designed by Cai Rong
Art by Wang Xianchun and Wen Jingen

Chinese Running Script Calligraphy for Beginners

ISBN 978-7-119-04860-4
© 2007 by Foreign Languages Press
Published by Foreign Languages Press
24 Baiwanzhuang Road, Beijing, 100037, China
Home page: http://www.flp.com.cn
Email address: info@flp.com.cn
sales@flp.com.cn
Distributed by China International Book Trading Corporation
35 Chegongzhuang Xilu, Beijing 100044, China
P. O. Box 399, Beijing, China

Printed in the People's Republic of China

Contents

Translator's notes:

1. All illustrations in this book were executed and provided by the author unless otherwise stated. 书中未注明作者的图片均为本书作者所作。

2. To make this book more accessible for non-Chinese readers, the translator has extensively edited the original text, and added some illustrations. The translator, and not the author, is responsible for all errors accruing from any rewriting and rearrangement.

为适应外国读者需要，本书编译过程中对原作的图文做了一定改动。着粪续貂，在所难免；所生舛误，咎在译者。敬希作者及读者见谅。

Panel inscribed by
Emperor Qianlong
(1711 — 1799) in
Tanzhe Temple,
Western outskirts of
Beijing

Dragon-gate couplet

Panel of the artist's shop Qing Mi Ge inscribed by Wu Changshuo (1844 — 1927)

Poem of Huang Bi written
in his own hand

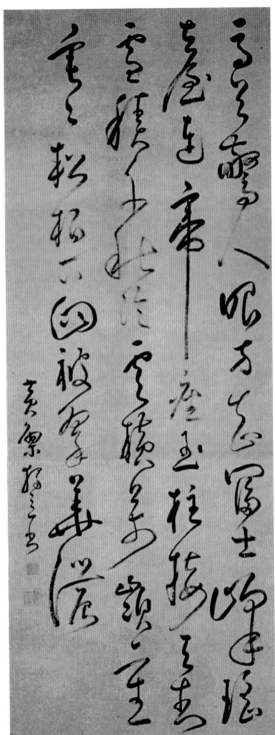

Calligraphic works are indispensable items in road-side cheap stands.

The top of a gateway in a village of Northern China

This small shop writes names in Chinese for non-Chinese customers.
photographs pp 5-11 by Wen Jingen

Inscription on rock in a mountain

Letter by Tang Yin (1470 — 1523)

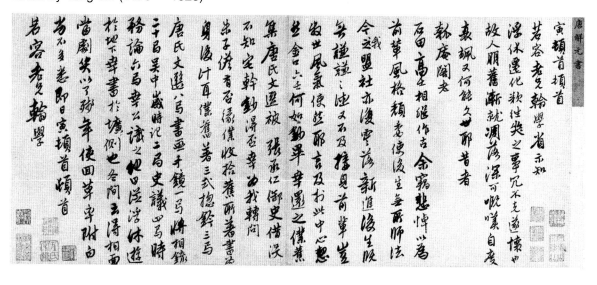

Chinese Running Script Calligraphy for Beginners

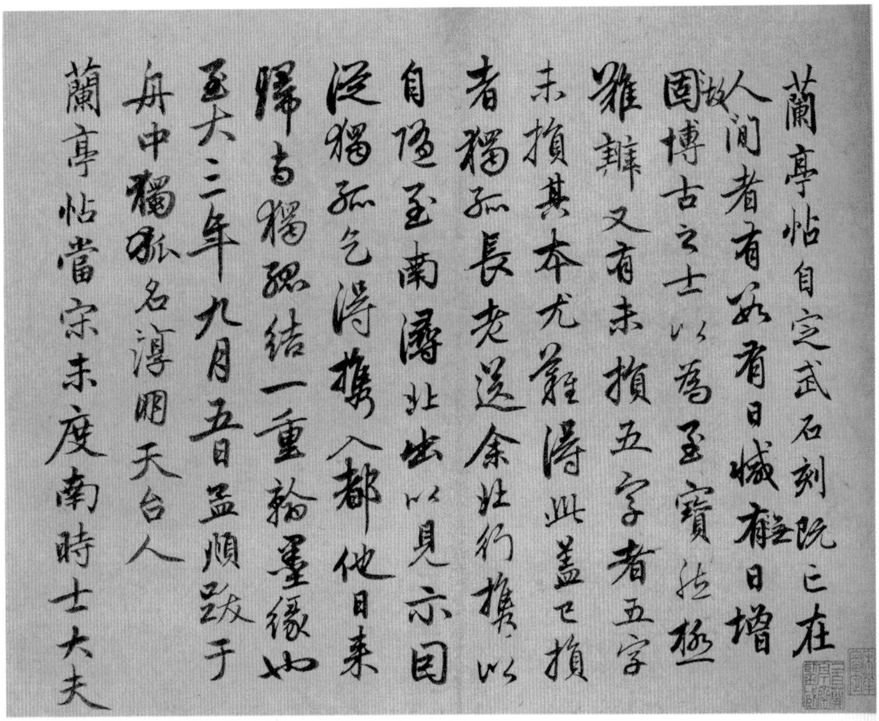

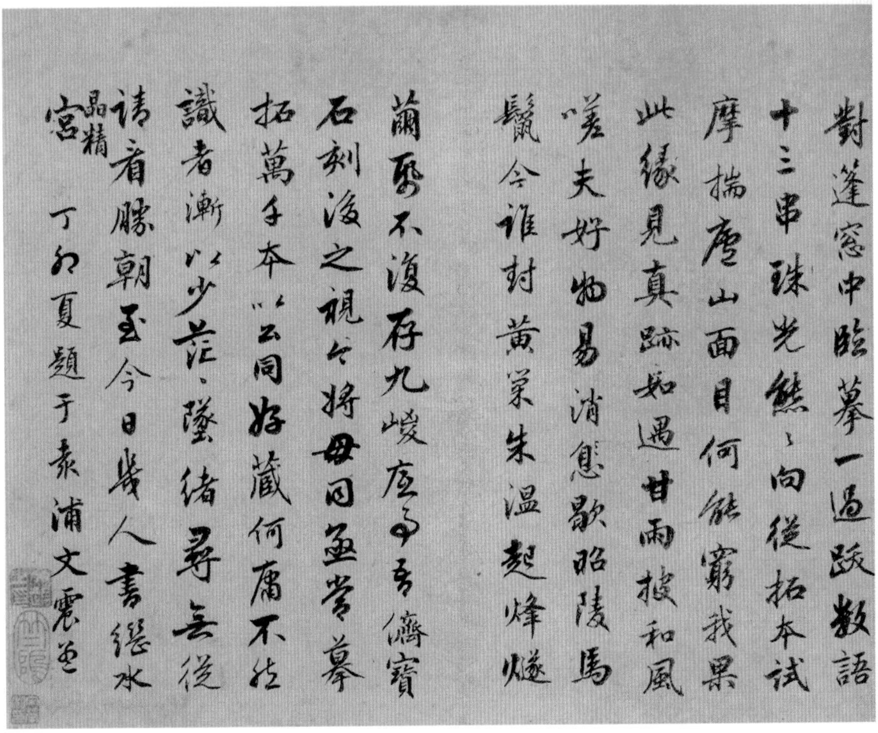

蘭亭帖自定武石刻既已在
人間者有數有日減無日增
故博古之士以為至寶然極
難辨又有未損五字者為至
寶則又難得此蓋已損五字
者獨孤長老送余壯行攜以
自隨至南潯北出以見示因
浸獨孤乞得攜入都他日來
歸吾獨孤結一重翰墨緣如
至大三年九月五日孟順跋于
舟中獨孤名淳朋天台人
蘭亭帖當宗末度南時士大夫

對蓬窗中臨摹一過跋數語
十三串珠光熊熊向後拓本試
摩挲唐山面目何能窮我累
此緣見真跡如遇甘雨披和風
嗟夫好物易消憩昭陵馬
髯今誰村黃棠朱溫起烽燧
蘭亭不復存九嶷虞子号齎寶
石刻後之視之將毋同嘗摹
拓萬千本以云同好藏何庸不朽
識者漸以少荒墜緒尋無後
請看勝朝至今日巻人書繾水
晶精宮　丁卯夏題于泰浦文震孟書

by Wen Zhenmeng
(1574 — 1636)

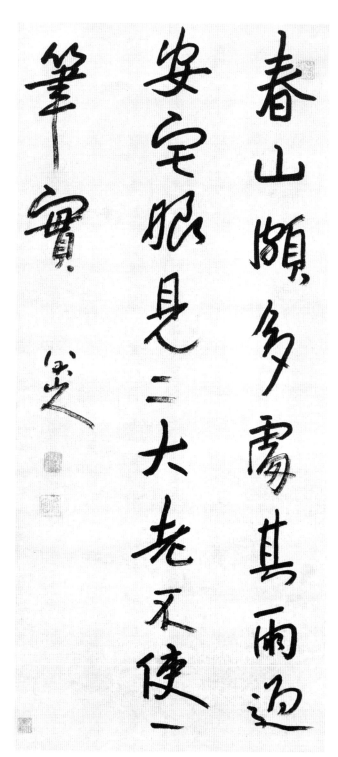

by Zhu Da (also known as Bada Shanren, 1626 — 1705)

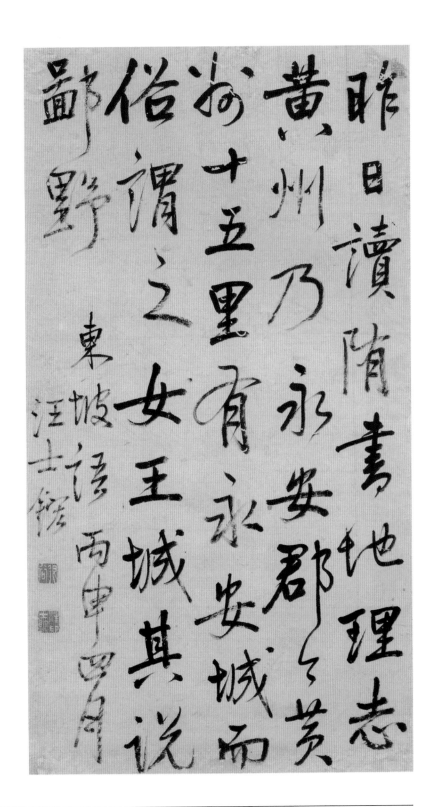

昨日讀隋書地理志黃州乃永安郡黃岡十五里有永安城而俗謂之女王城其說鄙野

東坡語丙申四月

汪士鋐

by Wang Shihong, 1716

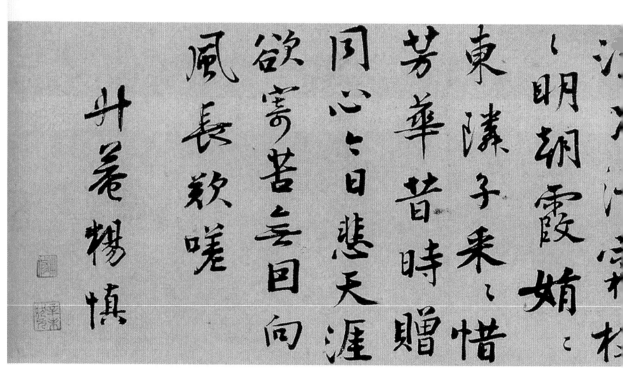

by Yang Shen (1488 — 1559)

Chinese Running Script Calligraphy for Beginners

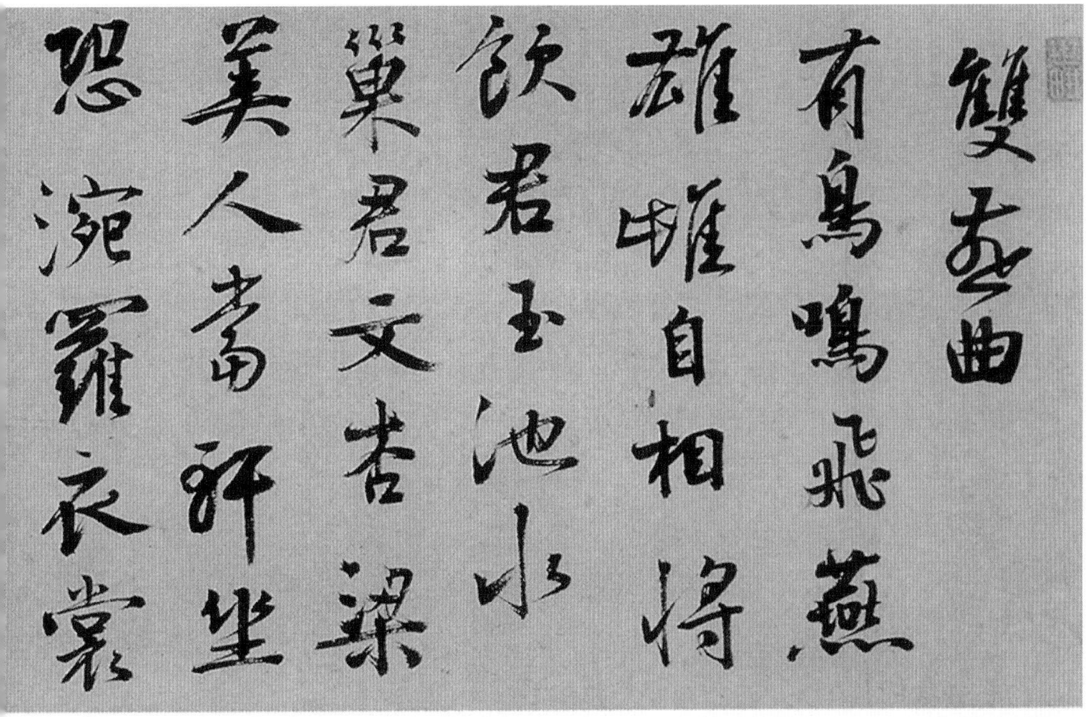

雙白鵠

有鳥鳴飛燕
雌雄自相將
巢君文杏梁
飲君玉池水
美人當軒坐
恐婉罷衣裳

主人華屋恩
雜忘頭主歲
千歲、、巢君
堂
涉江采芙蓉
沉、秩江水灼
、芙蓉花葉、、

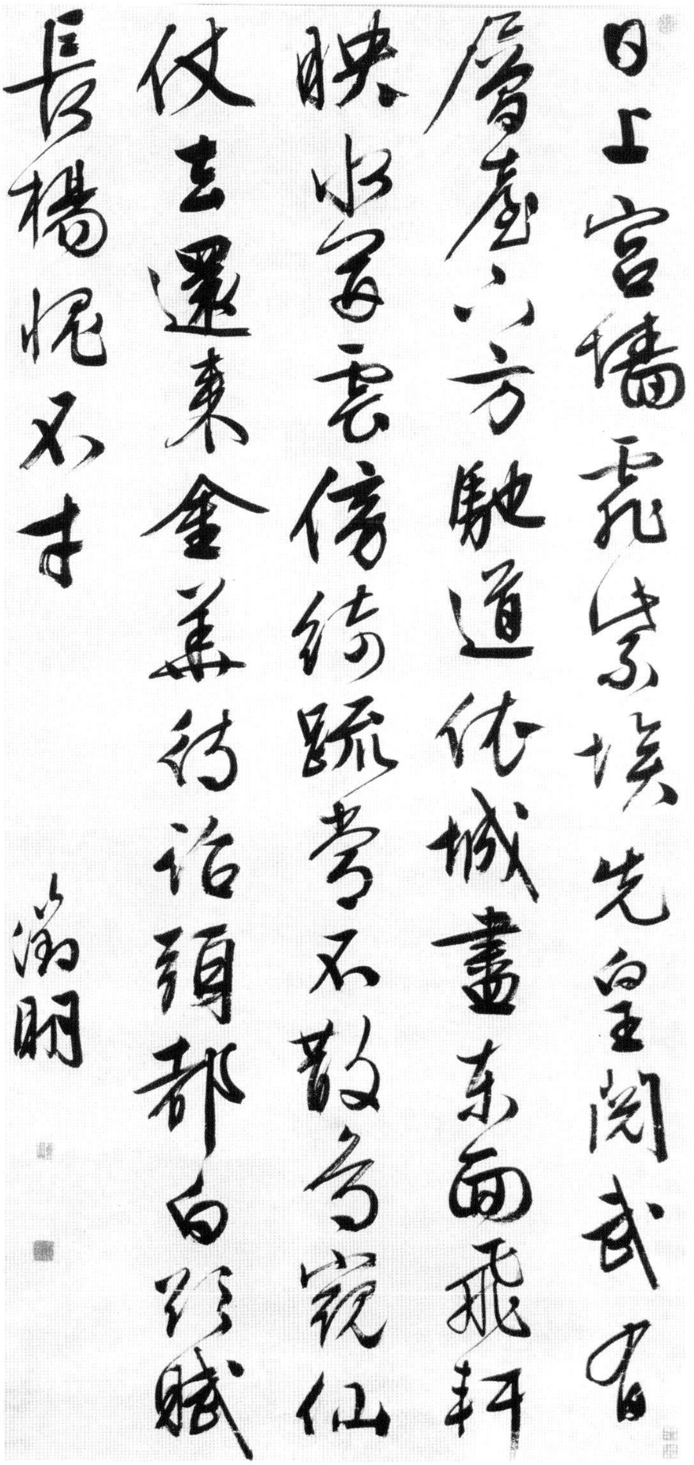

日上宫墙凫霭先皇阁武昌

层台八方驰道依城尽东面飞斗

映水层云傍绮疏夸不敌兮窥仙

仗去还东金茎药谒头都白龙赋

长桥恍不才

徵明

by Wen Zhengming (1470 — 1559)

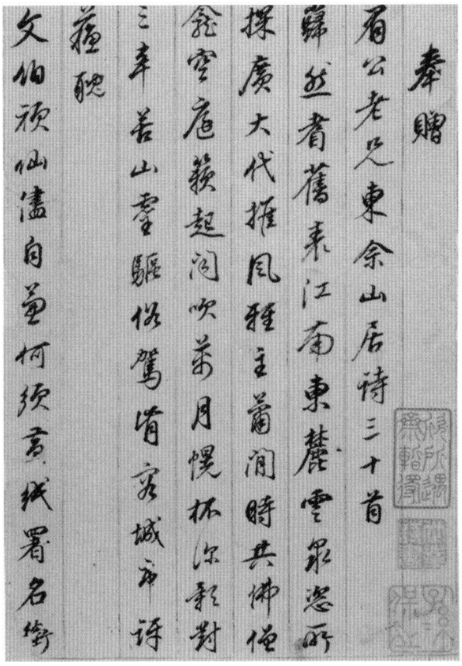

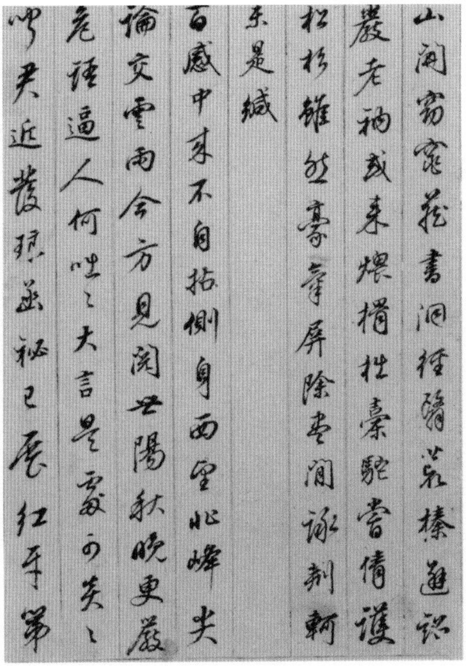

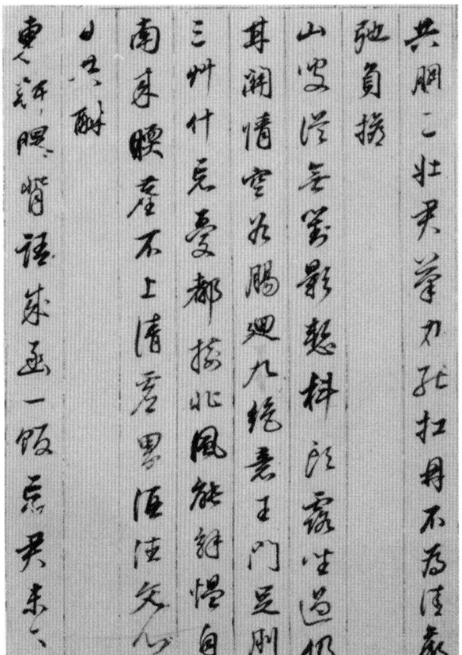

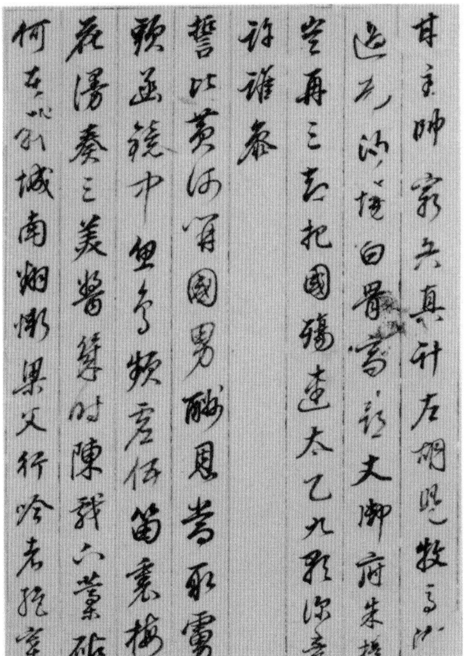

by Dong Qichang (1555 — 1636)

by Yong Xing, 1810

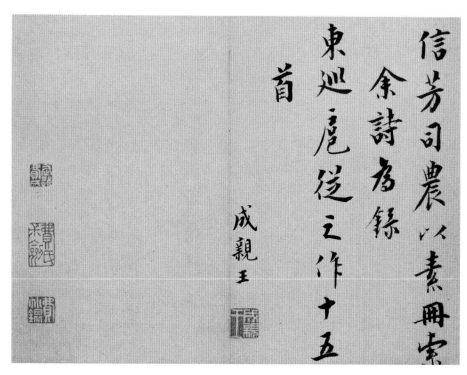

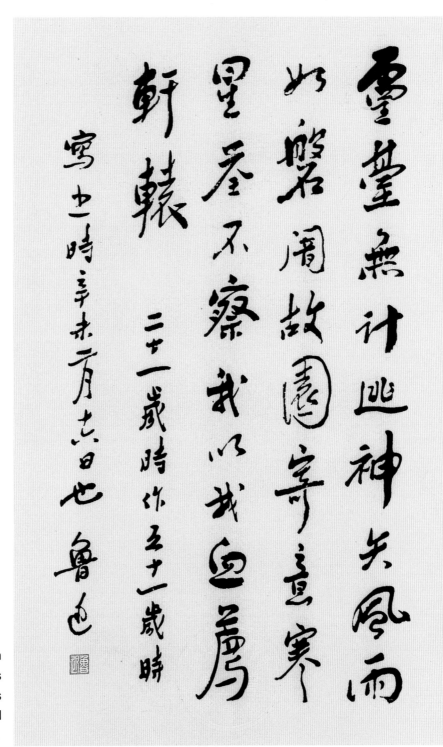

靈臺無計逃神矢，風雨如磐闇故園。寄意寒星荃不察，我以我血薦軒轅

二十一歲時作 五十一歲時

寫出時辛未二月志日也 魯迅

A poem by Lu Xun
(1881 — 1936) in his
own hand. Lu Xun is
a great thinker and
writer.

Introduction

Wen Jingen

I suppose you have learnt some Chinese language and may have developed an interest in Chinese calligraphy. In textbooks of Chinese language you see the print types like this:

Also, the "regular printing type" which is akin to your handwriting:

While a calligrapher's work may be like this:

Illustration by Wen Jingen

This form of calligraphy is called regular script or *kaishu* 楷书 [書]. As its name suggests, it has been regularly used especially in formal or official documents. This style of calligraphy has the advantage of being easily recognizable, but the disadvantage is that you cannot write it quickly. Like other peoples in the world, the ancient Chinese did not always work slowly. A poet had a sudden inspiration and needed to write the verses formed in his head immediately; a clerk must note down a dictation as fast as the superior spoke; a doctor may have to give a quick prescription. To meet this need, ancient Chinese people invented a fast handwriting cursive script or as a word-for-word translation, "grass calligraphy" 草书[書].

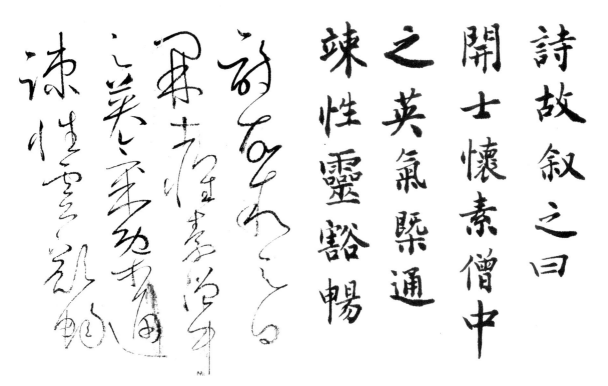

Cursive script by Huai Su (c. AD 725 — 785)

Huai Su's cursive scripts translated into regular scripts (by Wen Jingen)

You can imagine that the writer completed the work at a dash. But this style of calligraphy has a drastic disadvantage — untrained eyes can hardly recognize the characters. Compare the characters in cursive script and their counterpart in regular script and you will see the problem.

To overcome the slow execution of regular script and unidentifiable nature of cursive script, a calligraphic style in between is preferred. It is the running script, or *xingshu* 行书[書]. This style of calligraphy is quickly executable and at the same time the result is easily recognizable.

Illustration by Wen Jingen

If you have not yet learnt regular script calligraphy, I recommend that you learn it first. There is a text book on regular script calligraphy in our series. If you have already learnt regular script calligraphy, it is high time you studied the running script. Once you master this style of calligraphy, you will write a beautiful hand at a fairly quick speed. Your efforts will reward you — so pick up your brush!

Exact resemblance to model characters is not achievable

In this book we recommend copying model characters from copybooks in order to learn. This has been proven as an efficient method. The learner should model his or her handwriting on the characters in the copybooks. By this exercise the student of calligraphy will gradually correct his or her bad writing habits and make progress. But the student should also be aware that a hundred-percent resemblance of his or her writing to the model characters is out of the question. Ancient Chinese calligraphers discovered that a style of calligraphy is determined by a person's disposition and a calligrapher cannot even pass his style to his offspring (虽在父兄不能移子弟). If one could make an exact reproduction of another person's calligraphy, a signature could not be used as evidence in legal procedures.

The following picture shows Wang Xizhi's calligraphic work as seen in a calligrapher's copy.

The following is the rubbing of another copy done by the celebrated calligrapher Ouyang Xun:

Compare the stroke at the triangle sign. In this copy the stroke has a square beginning while in the other copy it is sharp. This in fact reveals the copier's own style. Look at Ouyang Xun's own calligraphy where a horizontal stroke usually has square ends.

Tools

The brush

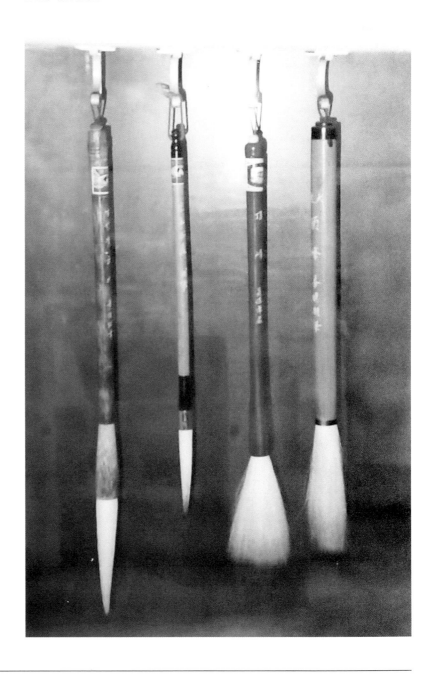

Brushes can be divided into three categories: (1) soft-fibre brushes, (2) stiff-fibre brushes and (3) mixed-fibre brushes.

A soft-fibre brush is made of goat hair. In Chinese it is called *yang hao* 羊毫. The brush made of cock feather (*ji hao* 鸡[鷄]毫) also belongs to this category but it is not as often used as *yang hao*.

A stiff-fibre brush is made of hare or weasel hair, called in Chinese *zi hao* 紫毫 or *lang hao* 狼毫.

A mixed-fibre brush is made of more than one hair. This kind of brush is neither too soft nor too stiff. It is good for beginners and especially for writing running script. In Chinese such brushes are called *jianhao* 兼毫. Brushes of this type include *da baiyun* 大白云[雲] (large white cloud), *zhong baiyun* 中白云[雲] (medium white cloud), *xiao baiyun* 小白云[雲] (small white cloud), *wu zi wu yang* 五紫五羊(five parts hare five parts goat), *qi zi san yang* 七紫三羊 (seven parts hare three parts goat), etc.

The size of your brush is determined by the size of strokes desired.

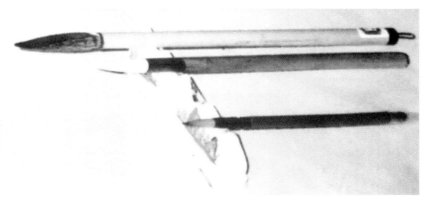

Different sizes of brushes

In terms of the length of the brush-tip, brushes can be divided into long-fibre brushes and short-fibre brushes. Calligraphers can choose either or both according to their writing practice or habit. Personally, I prefer long-fibre brushes.

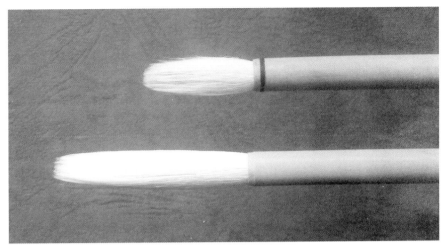

Short-fibre brush and long-fibre brush, photograph by Wen Jingen

Choosing a good brush

A good brush should have a straight shaft and fibres that have "four virtues": sharp pointed, flush, circular and resilient.

Sharp pointed: when the brush is wet, it is sharply pointed;

Bad brush   Good brush

Flush: when the brush is pressed flat, the end of fibres forms a straight line;

Bad brush   Good brush

Round: the brush fibres should be in a conic form; the outline of the brush should be a perfect circle;

Resilient: after pressing the brush and then raising it, the brush will resume its former shape.

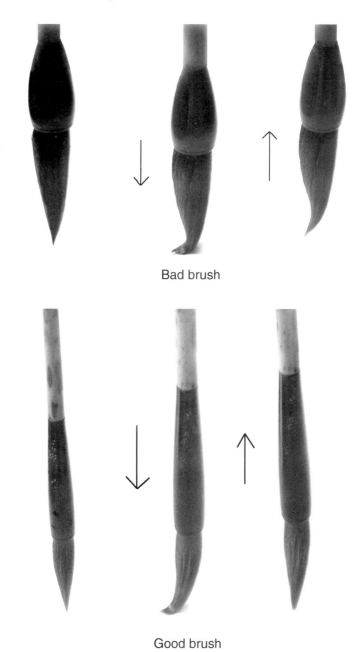

Bad brush

Good brush

Illustrations by Wen Jingen

Using a new brush

If a new brush has a tip with fibres unglued, just use it. First wet the brush thoroughly in clean water, squeeze out the water, then load it with ink and write.

If, however, a new brush has a tip whose fibres are sealed with alum or resin (for purpose of safe transportation), you can hold the brush, knead it from the tip to the heel with your thumb and forefinger until the hairs from the middle to the point of the brush become loosened. Then dip the brush in half a cup of water, leaving it in the water for a while until the alum or resin in the tip is removed. You can now use it.

Always stroke the brush across a palette, tile or the lid of the ink stone to make sure all fibres lie adjacent to each other and a good point is formed.

If after stroking your brush, you still have surplus liquid; remove this excess by stroking the brush on a piece of tissue paper.

Washing your brush

After use, you must wash your brush. You can leave it to dry horizontally. Better still, hang it downward on a brush hanger and leave it to dry. You must straighten the hairs, otherwise the fibres in the brush will become awry and the brush will not perform well.

The ink

In the past Chinese people ground an ink stick on an ink stone to produce ink. Nowadays most people use ready-made liquid ink. Quality ink brands are *yi de ge* 一得阁[閣], *zhonghua* 中华[華] (China), *Cao Sugong* 曹素功 and others. When you use such ink, pour some from the bottle onto the ink stone or a plate. If the ink is too thick, you can pick up a little water with your brush or add some water on the ink stone, but you must not add water to your bottle. Watered ink tends to stink or go bad.

Paper

The best paper for Chinese calligraphy is of course xuan paper *xuan zhi* 宣纸[紙]. But *xuan* paper is expensive. For beginners, usable papers are cheap grass paper, *maobian zhi* 毛边[邊]纸 and *yuanshu zhi* 元书[書]纸. Other types of paper are usable too so long as the surface of the paper is water absorbent and is not slippery.

The ink stone

The ink stone is used to grind the ink stick, hold the ground ink and to stroke the brush fibres on so as to make them straight and adjacent to

each other. An ink stone may be made of only one piece of stone, or with a lid (of the same or different material as the base). Since nowadays Chinese calligraphers seldom grind an ink stick to produce ink, the ink stone is not as important as before. Some calligraphers use a dish instead. After using, you must wash your ink stone clean.

Ink stone with a lid, photograph by Wen Jingen

Felt

A piece of felt under your paper will absorb the ink running through the paper. Without this piece of felt, the ink will run through, stick your paper to the table and spoil your writing.

Holding the Brush

Sitting

Hold your head square, keep your back straight, hold your arm above the paper and put your feet comfortably on the ground. Hold the brush with your right hand and press on the paper with your left hand.

Standing

Bow your head a little to look at the paper, relax your body, and reach out your arms. Stand steady with your feet the same distance apart as the width between your shoulder blades.

Hold the brush with your five fingers

You usually hold a pen or pencil with three fingers. To hold the brush your five fingers must work in concert. Look at the picture: your thumb applies an outward force on the brush shaft, your forefinger applies a force inwardly, your middle finger reinforces your forefinger, your ring finger pushes the brush shaft and the little finger reinforces the ring finger. Leave an empty cave in your palm — imagine you are holding an egg in your hand. If you hold the brush shaft with a fist, you cannot move the brush freely. Do not hold the brush shaft too firmly or too loosely. The position of your hand on the brush shaft is determined by the size of the characters you are writing. The larger the characters you are writing, the higher your hand should be on the shaft. There is no hard and fast rule.

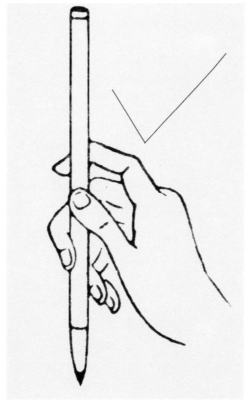

Hold the brush this way.

Do not hold the brush like this.

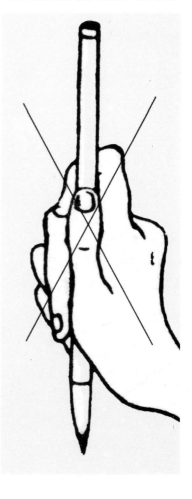

Move the brush with your wrist

To control the movement of a brush, you must coordinate your fingers, wrist and elbow. You hold the brush with your fingers and control the movement of the brush mainly with your wrist and elbow.

To write small characters, your right wrist rests on the table or on your left hand, as the picture shows.

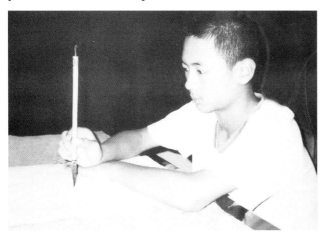

To write medium-sized characters (3-6 cm across), raise your right wrist.

To write larger characters, raise your elbow and wrist.

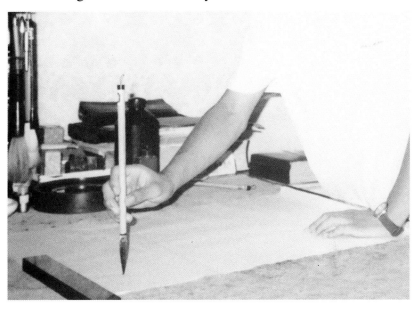

To write very large characters (larger than 15 cm), hold the brush this way.

The difference between pen calligraphy and brush calligraphy:

While you move your brush, you sometimes lift it and at other times press it, producing strokes in various thickness that you cannot achieve with a pen.

If the brush moves slowly on the paper, ink will run into paper quickly. Poor control over the brush movement on the paper will produce large inkblots. When the brush skips over the paper, the ink produces fleeting traces. If the brush moves at the proper speed, ink will be absorbed into the paper to give the desired result. Therefore deliberate moist or dry strokes will be achieved. With a pen you cannot achieve such strokes.

As you manipulate the brush, you can keep the brush tip at the centre of the stroke you are doing. Thus the central part of a stroke takes more ink than its edges and hence the central part of a stroke is darker than the edges. Such a stroke looks full and three-dimensional. You cannot produce such strokes with a pen.

When you write with a pen, only the end of the nib touches the paper; the other part of a pen never touches. When you write with a brush, not only the point, but also the middle part of the brush tip is often used.

The special way of holding the brush enables you raise and press the brush with more strength applied or sometimes with less strength to give a required effect.

Brush calligraphy and pen calligraphy,
illustration by Wen Jingen

Copying Model Characters from a Copybook

Practice makes perfect

The best way to learn running script calligraphy is to copy from a copybook. Choose a good version and copy from it every day. It is better to exercise at fixed hours — in the morning, evening or night, depending on what time is free for you. It is better to write a certain number of characters every day. For a beginner 30 to 50 characters may be a good number. Do not write too many or too few. Try to finish it in an hour. Persist in regular exercise and you will make rapid progress.

Do not swap horses while crossing the stream. It is not wise to change the copybook before you have learnt its style. Do not begin to imitate a new copybook until you can imitate the style of an old copybook without looking at it.

Date your exercises. When you look at your old homework, you will see the great progress you have made over a period of time and will be more confident.

While copying from a copybook, you must study the characters carefully before you set your brush on the paper. You can study individual strokes, the whole structure of a character and echoing of different strokes.

Tracing can be done in three ways:

(1) Place a piece of half-transparent paper over the model characters (if possible, put the paper on a designer's table) and write by covering the image of the model characters.

(2) Trace the outline of the model characters with a pencil and fill the outline with a brush loaded with ink. You must fill the outline of one stroke with one brushstroke. Do not fill the outline of one stroke with many strokes as you do in a colouring book.

(3) Trace the strokes of the model characters by drawing a line along the central part of strokes.

There is a misunderstanding that only beginners trace copybooks. Good calligraphers do often trace from copybooks and rubbings from ancient tablet inscriptions as well. By tracing model characters, a calligrapher will learn more about the movement and echoing of strokes of ancient masters.

Copying and tracing are a basic form of training for calligraphers.

Study the copybook

The success of copying and tracing lies in study of copybooks. If you copy from a copybook in a "writing a stroke as you see it" manner, the strokes you produce tend to be different from those in the copybook. By studying a copybook you will have a better understanding of the strokes and characters. Only with a better understanding of what you are copying, will you make a better copy.

What to study. You should study how a stroke begins and ends — its width, length and direction. You should also study the structure of a character: which part is larger or higher than the other, which strokes go first and which after. Thirdly, you must study the arrangement of characters on a calligraphic piece. Finally, you can study the variation of strokes. Try to find out the sequence of strokes in a character. Pay special attention to the beginning and turnings in a stroke.

We cannot see the ancient masters using their brush to execute a calligraphic work, but by studying their work we can get close to an understanding of how they wrote those characters. This will increase our understanding of calligraphy and increase our interest in it. A calligrapher who often studies copybooks tends to be a good appraiser of calligraphy.

Brushstrokes

The head of a brush is divided into the following parts: the tip, the middle section (belly) and the heel.

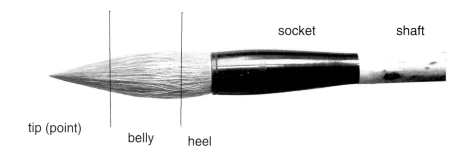

socket   shaft

tip (point)   belly   heel

Photograph by Wen Jingen

When the brush tip is used, the fibres at the point lie close to each other. When the brush moves on the paper, it is often pressed down and then the fibres in middle section spread. The more force is applied, the wider the fibres spread. When the brush is lifted, the fibres will come together again. Never let the brush tip leave the paper until a stroke is finished.

Never press the brush heel onto the paper, otherwise the fibres in the brush will not recover their shape and the brush is no more usable.

Controlling the brush

Hold the brush vertically and keep the brush tip in the centre of the stroke it produces. This kind of stroke is called "centre-tip stroke" or *zhongfeng* 中锋[鋒].

If the brush tip is at one edge of the stroke, it is side-tip stroke or *cefeng* 侧锋.

A centre-tip stroke

A side-tip stroke

Centre-tip stroke (top) and side-tip stroke (bottom), with the white line showing the position of the brush point (in actual writing the white line does not exist).

Since ancient times, most calligraphers consider that a centre-tip stroke is preferable. Some calligraphers do use side-tip strokes to achieve a special result. For beginners, centre-tip is the norm.

A way to keep the brush tip at the centre of the stroke is to begin a stroke by a small movement in the opposite direction to that of the whole stroke. Raising the brush and putting it down again will achieve centre-tip stroke too.

Begin a stroke by moving the brush tip against the direction of the stroke.

The trace of the brush tip can be concealed or exposed.

Bring the brush tip back again at the end of a stroke so as to conceal the brush tip within the stroke.

Remember: to achieve a stroke with the trace of the brush point concealed, you have to

Start/end a stroke to the right by moving the brush tip to the left;

Start/end a stroke to the left by moving the brush tip to the right;

Start/end a downward stroke by moving the brush tip upward, and

Start/end an upward stroke by moving the brush tip downward.

In short: you have to *start / end a stroke by moving the brush tip in the direction opposite to the direction of the stroke.*

A stroke produced in this way looks full and hefty.

On the other hand, a stroke with the trace of the brush tip exposed looks nimble and spirited.

Different ways of starting and ending a stroke produce a sharp, oblique, square or round end of good looking strokes.

Starting a stroke:

You can start a stroke either by leaving its tip exposed or concealed.

Brush tip exposed at the beginning of a stroke

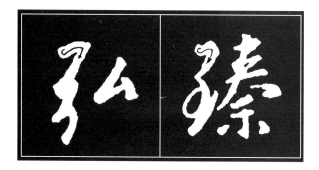

Conceal the brush tip at the beginning of a stroke

Ending a stroke:

Likewise, you can also end a stroke by leaving the trace of the brush tip exposed or concealed.

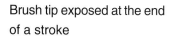
Brush tip exposed at the end of a stroke

Sometimes you need to lift the brush (but do not take the brush off the paper) so as to produce a thinner stroke or the thinner part of a stroke.

1. Start a stroke by conceiling the brush tip

2. Press the brush and turn the brush tip

3. Move the brush keeping the brush tip at the centre of the stroke

4. Raise the brush tip a little

5. Press the brush tip

6. End the stroke by turning the brush tip backward

Execution of a stroke

Sometimes you need to press down with the brush so as to produce a broader stroke or a broader part of a stroke. This technique is often used at the end of right-falling strokes.

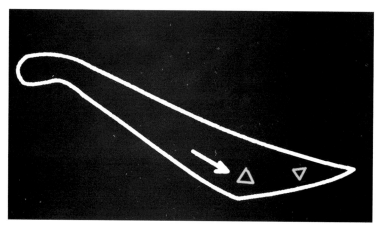

The brush is pressed down (at the triangle on the left) and then lifted (at the reversed triangle on the right).

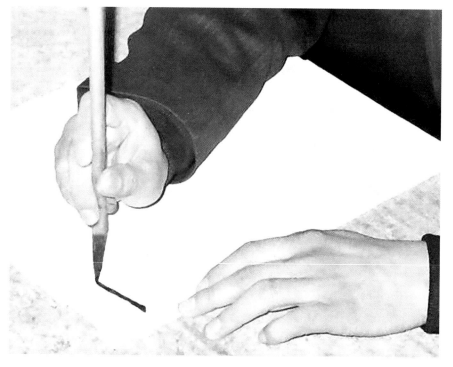

Lift the brush

Press the brush

Lift the brush

Round-turning

While producing a bending stroke, do not turn the brush shaft with your fingers. Conceal the trace of brush tip and move the brush at an even speed. A stroke produced in this way looks vigorous and suggestive.

Round-end stroke

Such a stroke is produced by concealing the trace of the brush tip. Without any edge exposed, such a stroke looks ample.

Sharp-turning

Square-end stroke

Employing the technique of sharp-turning, you can produce square-end strokes. A square-end stroke looks forceful and imposing. Use of round-end and square-end strokes will make the running script calligraphy more rhythmic.

Thirsty stroke

If the brush contains little ink or moves quickly, a thirsty stroke may be produced. Such strokes often appear in running and cursive script calligraphy. They look bold and impetuous.

Understanding Running Script Characters

Comparison of calligraphic styles

The poet and artist Su Shi (1037-1101) makes a good comparison of different calligraphic styles: "Regular script is like a standing man, running script, a walking man and cursive script a dashing man." This suggests that running script shows impetuses and great varieties of strokes and structures.

(1) Some running script characters are rather "regular".

Running script   Regular script

Illustration by Wen Jingen

Remember: do not write running script too "regularly" or some characters will look "out of place" in the whole calligraphic work.

(2) Sometimes cursive script characters or cursive script style may be used in a running script calligraphic work.

Characters from a "running script" calligraphic work:

Running script for these characters:

Cursive script for these characters:

Regular script for these characters:

(3) Joining strokes. The beginning of a stroke is often joined with the end of the previous stroke. These links make the whole work more coherent and vivid.

Running   Regular

Regular   Running

Sometimes circles and holes are left among the joining strokes that make the whole work livelier. But too many such circles will make the calligraphic work flashy.

(4) Echoing broken strokes looks like two birds eyeing and calling to each other. Such a relationship appears between strokes within a character, between two radicals of a character or between two characters.

(5) Upright and slanting radicals. The contrast of upright and slanting parts keeps running script calligraphy balanced in movement. One part slanting in one direction is countered by the other part slanting in the opposite direction. The whole character should be upright.

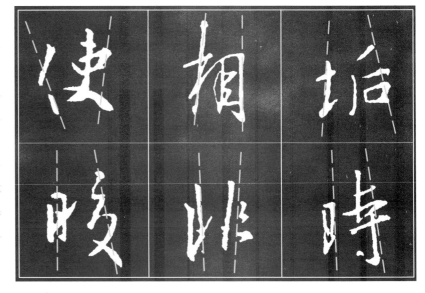

Do not set out to achieve slanting strokes. Avoid parallel strokes.

(6) Leaving out some strokes.

(7) Substituting square turnings with round ones. While producing such rounded strokes, the brush must be intentionally raised and lowered at certain places within the stroke, otherwise the stroke will become effeminate.

Strokes

Strokes in running script calligraphy show more variation than those in the regular script. Let us begin with individual strokes.

Dot *dian* 点[點]

Ancient Chinese calligraphers compared a dot to a "rock falling down a high mountain". In executing a dot, the calligrapher usually leaves the trace of the brush tip exposed.

Dots occurring at different positions within a character have different names and are produced in different ways.

(1) On the top of a character:

(2) On the left side:

(3) On the right:

(4) Raising dot:

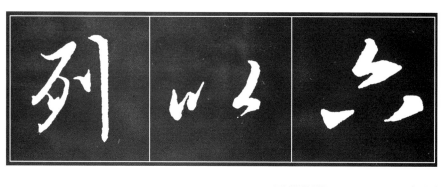

(5) Long dot:

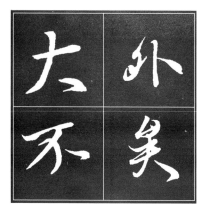 

(6) A radical consisting of two dots:

One dot above the other: the two dots are usually joined;

One dot beside the other: the two dots should echo each other and the dot on the right is usually larger than the left one. During execution of such dots, pressing the brush is often necessary.

Two dots at the left side of a character: The second dot is in a rising posture and larger than the one above it. Finish the second dot quickly and forcefully.

(7) A radical consisting of three dots: One must make the three dots echo each other. The last dot usually contains a turning movement of the brush tip.

Various ways of writing the radical of three dots in running script calligraphy. In regular script less varieties are found.

(8) Four dots at the bottom of a character.

(9) Paired dots.

Horizontal stroke *heng* 横

A horizontal stroke in Chinese calligraphy may be long or short. The longer one usually keeps a character in balance and the shorter one should be forceful. When several horizontal strokes appear in a character, they should be in varying angles and lengths.

Single horizontal stroke

(1) Horizontal stroke joining a lower stroke. Begin the stroke with the trace of the brush tip exposed, then press the brush slightly and end the stroke by turning the brush tip to the left.

(2) Horizontal stroke joining a stroke above. Begin the stroke with the brush tip exposed, press the brush slightly and end the stroke at a raised angle.

(3) Horizontal stroke joining a previous stroke at the beginning and the stroke following on from its end. The stroke usually ends with a small hook.

(4) Short horizontal stroke.

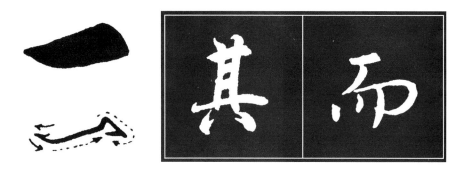

Parallel horizontal strokes

When several horizontal strokes appear in a character, write them in different lengths, widths and angles. Begin and end them in a different manner.

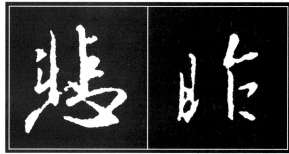

Vertical stroke *shu* 竖[豎]

A basic element in the Chinese character, the vertical stroke plays an important role in laying the centre of gravity of a character and in linking the previous to the successive characters. There are more ways of executing a vertical stroke in running script than in regular script calligraphy. In the regular script calligraphy, the vertical stroke is usually upright and vertical. In running script calligraphy, it can be in various angles and shapes.

(1) Single vertical stroke.

It may look like a "hanging needle", *xuan zhen* 悬针[懸針]. Start it by turning the brush tip upward, turn the brush downward and finish the stroke by lifting the brush off the paper gradually.

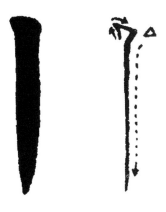

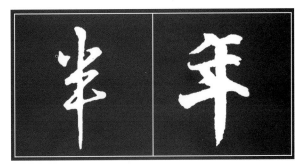

It may look like an "iron pillar", *tie zhu* 铁[鐵]柱. Start the stroke by turning the brush tip upward. At the end of the stroke, you should again turn the brush tip upward.

It may also look like a "falling dew drop", *chui lu* 垂露. Start the stroke directly and end it by turning the brush tip upward.

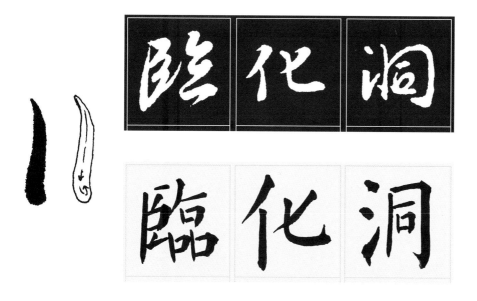

Arched vertical stroke, *hu shu* 弧竖. Start the stroke by turning the brush tip upward or leaving the brush tip at one side of the stroke, move the brush downward quickly and press the brush at the end of the stroke.

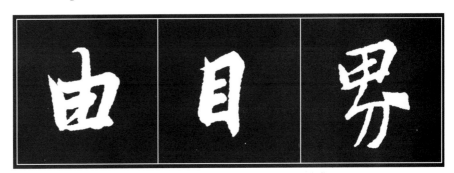

Oblique vertical stroke, *xie shu* 斜竖.

Hooked vertical stroke, *dai gou shu* 带钩竖. Sometimes a vertical stroke may have a hook to the left or right at its end.

(2) Parallel vertical strokes

When parallel vertical strokes appear in a character, they should be in different lengths and angles.

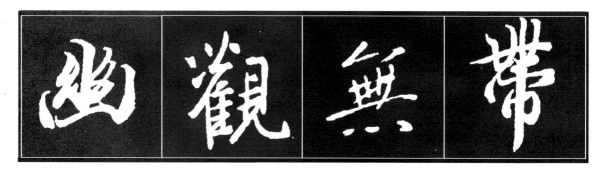

Left-falling stroke *pie* 撇

A left-falling stroke may be in different lengths and shapes, looking like a sword, a tusk or bird beak. Execute a left-falling stroke vigorously, smoothly but not flirtingly.

(1) Single left-falling stroke

Long left-falling stroke, *chang pie* 长[長]撇. Start it by turning the brush tip upward or leave the brush tip at one side of the stroke. Move the brush left downward while keeping the brush tip at the centre of the stroke. End the brush stroke quickly.

Short left-falling stroke, *duan pie* 短撇. Start the stroke by turning the brush tip and pressing the brush slightly. The stroke looks like a bird's beak. When there is a horizontal stroke under it, it should be more flat.

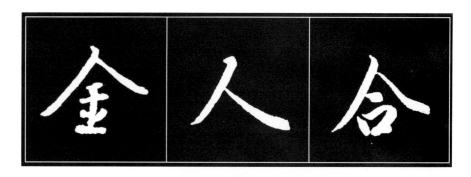

Vertical left-falling stroke, *zhi pie* 直撇. The upper half of the stroke is rather upright but the lower half tilts towards the left.

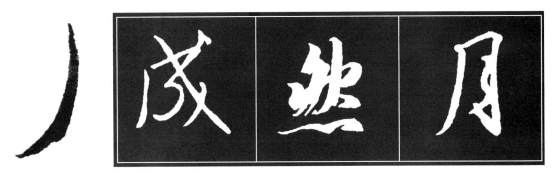

Long bending left-falling stroke, *chang qu pie* 长[長]曲撇. Such a stroke looks like a blade of the orchid, with the both ends slim.

Regular script for the two characters

Blunt left-falling stroke, *huifeng pie* 回锋[鋒]撇. The end of the stroke is executed by turning the brush tip backward.

Hooked left-falling stroke, *dai gou pie* 带钩[鈎]撇. The end of the stroke turns upright, forming a small hook. The hook should not be too long.

(2) Multiple left-falling strokes

When several left-falling strokes appear in a character, those strokes should be in various shapes and lengths. For example, the three left-falling strokes on the right of the character 形 are not parallel with each other nor the same length. The top stroke is reduced to an upward dot and the middle stroke changes into a vertical stroke. In the right hand of the character 及 the left-falling stroke on the left is straight and executed with the brush tip backward, and the left-falling stroke on the right is sharp-ended and bent.

Regular script for the two characters

Identical left-falling strokes in one character look monotonous. Always try to achieve variations by alternating the length, angle of the stroke, and the movement of the brush tip in the stroke. Compare the character 彭 and 畅 in the following illustration:

A left-falling stroke may be linked to other strokes or be separated from them.

Right-falling stroke *na* 捺

The right-falling stroke has many varieties. The right-falling stroke is often the final stroke of a character. So it exerts an important influence on the whole character or even the whole calligraphic work.

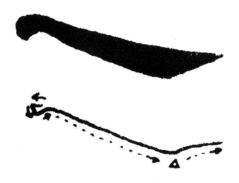

Slanting right-falling stroke, *xie na* 斜捺. The stroke moves down to the right. Begin the stroke gently and then apply some force on the brush, stop the brush and finally finish the stroke by drawing the brush off the paper, showing the trace of the brush tip.

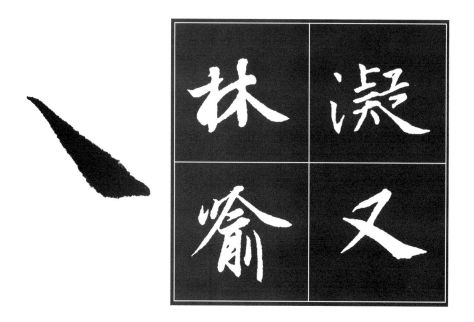

Horizontal right-falling stroke, *ping na* 平捺. This stroke is also known as "wave", *bo* 波. Start by moving the brush tip in the direction opposite to that of the stroke, raise the brush tip a little, move it down to the right and press the brush with increasing strength. At the end of the stroke, the brush stops a moment and then leaves the paper quickly whilst moving to the right. Sometimes the end of the stroke forms an upward hook.

Long right-falling dot, *changdian na* 长点[長點]捺 (also *fan na* 反捺). This stroke is an arch-formed long dot. Start the stroke gently and apply force increasingly as the brush moves to the right. Finish the stroke by turning the brush tip upwards and to the left.

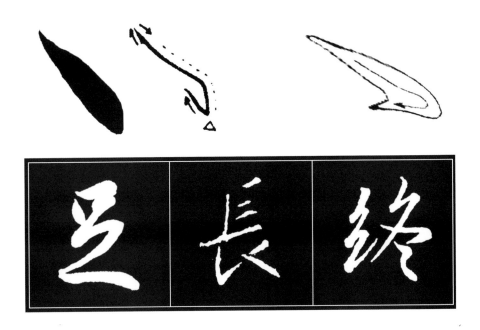

Blunt right-falling stroke, *hui feng na* 回锋[鋒]捺. When the brush tip moves to the end of the stroke, reverse the brush tip.

Rising stroke *ti* 提

Also known as *tiao* 挑, this stroke links the left and the right parts of a character. It may be a separate stroke or the trace formed by linked strokes.

(1) Individual rising stroke, *duan ti* 短 提. Begin the stroke by pressing the brush tip downwards and to the right, then move the brush upwards and to the right, raising it off the paper quickly.

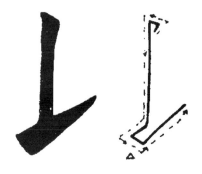

(2) Linked rising stroke, *chang ti* 长[長]提. The previous stroke moves downward and tilts to the left, turn to the right and upward.

Turning stroke, *zhe* 折

In regular script calligraphy a turning stroke usually has a sharp angle. In running script, it has a round turning. The turning should be spontaneous and natural.

(1) Vertical turning, *shu zhe* 竖[竪]折. At the turning the brush is raised a little and then moved to the right. At the end of the stroke, the brush tip can move backwards or not as you wish.

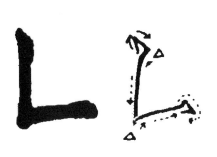

(2) Horizontal turning, *heng zhe* 横折. When the brush moves to the point of turning, stop the brush and press it before moving it downward. The brush tip moves upward at the end of the stroke.

(3) Slanting turning stroke, *xie zhe* 斜折.

(4) Round turning stroke, *yuan zhe* 圆[圓]折.

(5) Multiple turning stroke, *qu zhe* 曲折.

In regular script   In running script

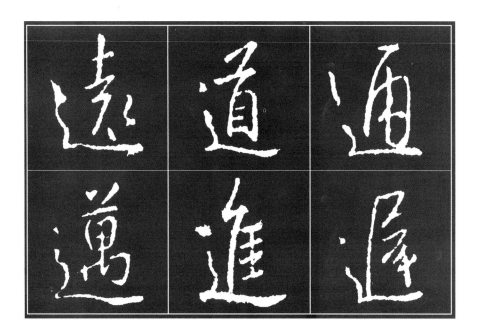

Notes: (1) When two turning strokes appear in one character, the upper one should be square and the lower one should be round.

(2) Sometimes a turning stroke is formed by joining two strokes.

(3) The multiple turning stroke is often simplified.

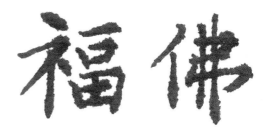

Illustration by Wen Jingen

(4) The round turning stroke is often used in place of a square turning stroke.

Illustration by Wen Jingen

Hook *gou* 钩

A hook can be compared to kicking where one must direct one's energy to the toes. In a like way, the end of the hook must be forceful.

Vertical hook, *shu gou* 竖钩.

Slanting hook, *xie gou* 斜钩.

Horizontal hook, *heng gou* 横钩.

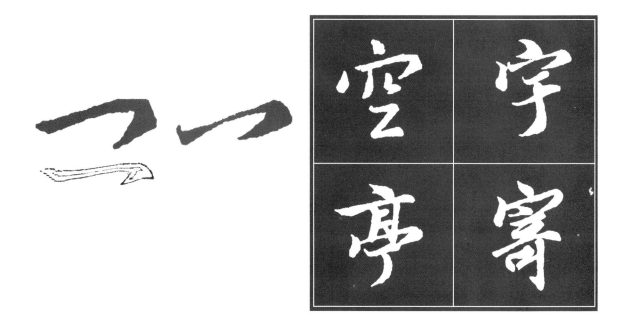

Bottom hook, *xin di gou* 心底钩. This stroke is the bottom of the character 心.

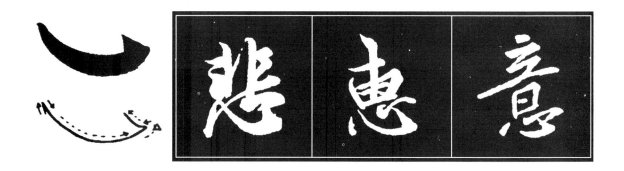

Vertical turning hook, *shu wan gou* 竖弯钩.

Blunt hook, *hui feng gou* 回锋钩. The brush tip is directed backwards at the end of the stroke.

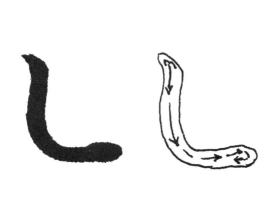

Horizontal turning hook, *heng zhe gou* 横折钩.

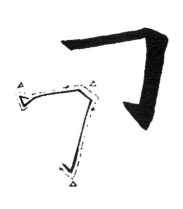

Right slanting hook, *heng zhe you xie gou* 横折右斜钩.

Notes: (1) A hook often joins to other strokes;

(2) the upper and lower parts and the left and right parts of a character should echo each other;

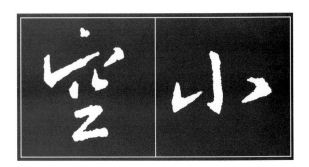

and (3) hooks in some characters are formed by joining of strokes — those hooks do not exist in the counterpart regular scripts characters.

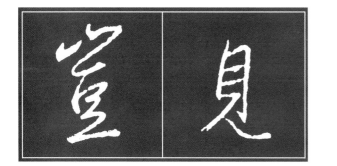 

Regular script

Structure

A Chinese character may be composed of one or more radicals. The configuration of the radicals appears in several ways.

Left-right:

Left-middle-right:

Top-bottom:

Top-middle-bottom:

Half-embracing:

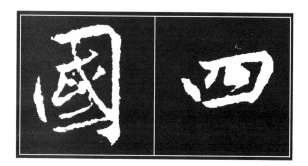

Complete embracing:

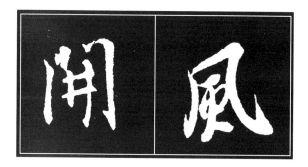

Left radicals

(1) Single man, *dan ren pang* 单人旁: 亻

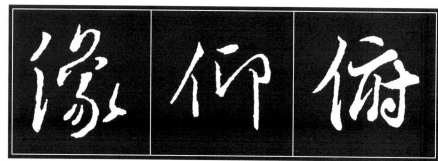

(2) Double man, *shuang ren pang* 双人旁：彳

(3) Three-dot water, *san dian shui* 三点水：氵

(4) Speech, *yan zi pang* 言字旁：言讠

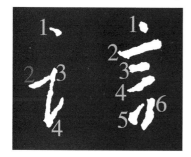 

(5) Left ear, *zuo erduo* 左耳朵：阝

(6) Standing heart, *shu xin pang* 竖心旁：忄

(7) Earth, *ti tu pang* 提土旁：土

(8) Woman, *nü zi pang* 女字旁：女

(9) Hand, *ti shou pang* 提手旁：扌

(10) Dog, *fan quan pang* 反犬旁 : 犭

(11) Sun, *ri zi pang* 日字旁 : 日

(12) Fire, *huo zi pang* 火字旁 : 火

(13) Vehicle, *che zi pang* 车字旁：车車

(14) Wood, *mu zi pang* 木字旁：木

(15) Horse, *ma zi pang* 马字旁：马馬

(16) King, *wang zi pang* 王字旁：王

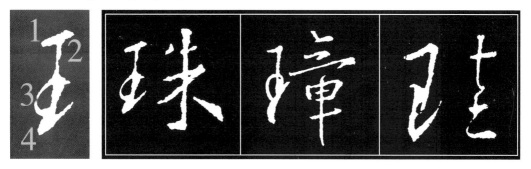

(17) Show, *shi zi pang* 示字旁：示礻

(18) Dress, *yi zi pang* 衣字旁：礻

(19) Stone, *shi zi pang* 石字旁：石

(20) Gold, *jin zi pang* 金字旁：金金

(21) Seedling, *he zi pang* 禾字旁：禾

(22) Rice, *mi zi pang* 米字旁：米

(23) Ear, *er zi pang* 耳字旁：耳

(24) Foot, *zu zi pang* 足字旁：足

(25) Bone, *gu zi pang* 骨字旁：骨

Right radicals

(1) See, *jian zi pang* 见字旁 : 见

(2) Moon, *yue zi pang* 月字旁 : 月

(3) Tapping, *fan wen pang* 反文旁 : 夂

(4) Page, *ye zi pang* 页字旁：页頁

(5) Owe, *qian zi pang* 欠字旁：欠

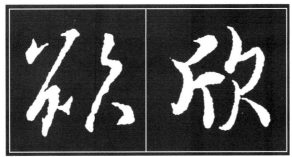

(6) Short-tailed bird, *zhui zi pang* 隹字旁：隹

(7) Ear on the right side, *you ergou* 右耳钩 : 阝

Top radicals

Usually the top radical is wider than the lower radical.

(1) Roof, *bao gai tou* 宝盖头 : 宀

(2) Mountain, *shan zi tou* 山字头：山

(3) Grass, *cao zi tou* 草字头：艹

(4) Rain, *yu zi tou* 雨字头：雨

Bottom radicals

(1) Child, *er zi di* 儿字底：儿

(2) Earth, *tu zi di* 土字底:土

(3) Shell, *bei zi di* 貝字底:貝

(4) Heart, *xin zi di* 心字底：心

(5) Container, *min zi di* 皿字底：皿

(6) Running Z, *zhou zhi di* 走字底：辶

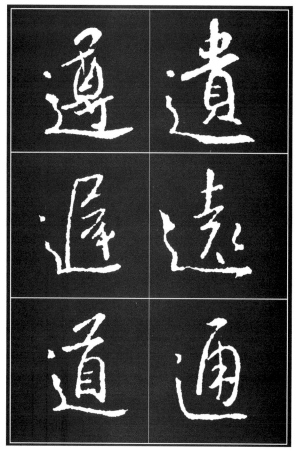

Try to make identical things different

In regular script calligraphy, the same character repeated in a piece of work appears largely the same. In running script calligraphy, however, one can achieve infinite variations of the same character by altering the execution of the strokes and the configuration of the structure. The great master calligrapher Wang Xizhi says: "When you execute a piece of calligraphy, you should make every character different and never make (identical characters) identical." The variation is achieved by employing different brushstrokes (some are gentle, others are forceful, some with the trace of the brush tip concealed, others with trace of brush tip exposed), different postures of strokes (some are straight, others curved), different configurations of strokes (some parts are crowded, others sparse, some parts are on the top, others at bottom) and an original arrangement of the whole page (some characters are large, others small, some long, others short etc.).

Making repeated radicals different

If two, three or occasionally four radicals are repeated in one character, try to make them look different by various means.

If the radical on the top and the one at the bottom are the same, the upper one is usually smaller than the lower one.

If the radical on the left and the one on the right are the same, write them in different sizes or shapes.

If a character contains three identical radicals, write these radicals in different postures and sizes.

Making repeated characters different

An outstanding example is Wang Xizhi's *Preface to the Poems at the Orchid Pavillion* (*Lanting Xu* 兰[蘭]亭序) in which the character 之 is repeated 21 times but none of them look the same.

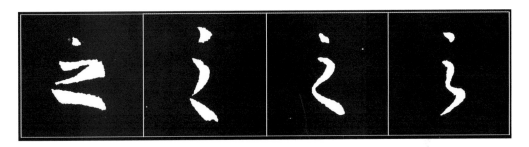

Other examples:

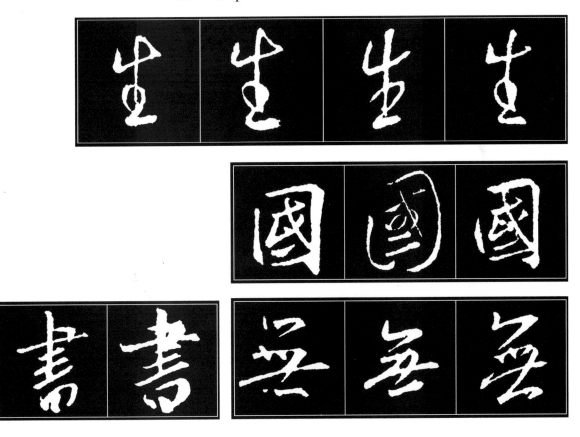

Altering the sequence of strokes

The principles governing the sequence of strokes in regular script calligraphy are:

(1) horizontal stroke before the vertical one;

(2) left-falling stroke before the right-falling stroke;

(3) from top to bottom;

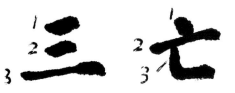

(4) from left to right;

(5) the outer strokes first;

(6) the inner part first;

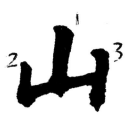

(7) closing the "gate" after everything has entered the "house";

(8) the middle part first.

Illustrations by Wen Jingen

By and large, these principles are observed in regular script calligraphy. But occasionally, calligraphers may alter the established stroke sequence for sake of convenience in the execution of running script calligraphy.

running
script

regular
script 1

regular 2

running
script

regular

running

regular

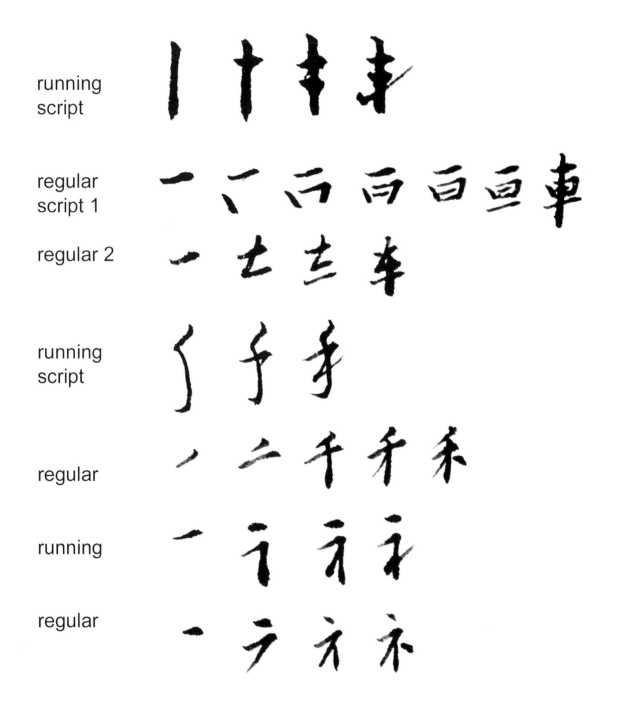

Illustrations by Wen Jingen

running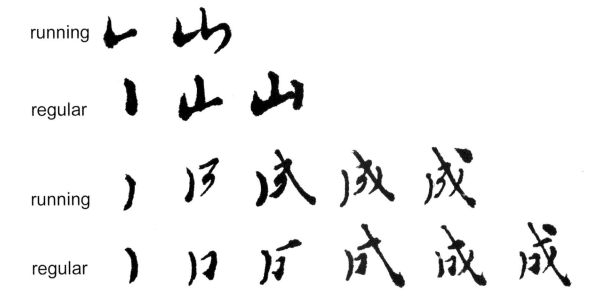

regular

running

regular

Illustrations by Wen Jingen

Make every character what it is

Chinese characters are not all of equal size, some are larger than others. In regular script calligraphy, the sizes of all characters are mainly the same. In running script, the difference in sizes of characters may be very large. Some characters may be extremely long while others are extremely short; some with dense strokes while others have sparse strokes. The different sizes and "postures" of various characters, like the variety of notes in music, produce a wonderful harmony.

Characters that end with a central vertical stroke look better if the last stroke is extended.

Characters consisting of two radicals, one above the other, should be written tall.

Characters with few strokes or short characters should be written short.

Characters consisting of two radicals, one beside the other, look better if one is lower than the other.

If a character has several radicals, write it large.

If the character has few strokes, write it small but do not write the strokes too densely.

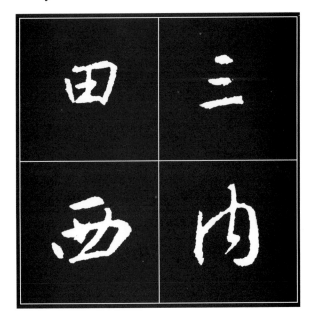

Some characters have few strokes, but they look large. Write them large.

Leave breathing room between the left and right radicals in the characters of left-right structure.

The characters with many strokes in top-bottom structure should be densely constructed.

And so should be the characters with left-right radicals and many strokes.

Giving way to each other

If a character has several radicals, they should give way to each other. Smaller radicals should give room for the larger ones. The larger ones should "embrace" the smaller ones. If one radical is long, the other radical should be short. If one radical is tall, the other should be shorter, and so on.

A narrow top over a wide bottom.

A broad top over a narrow bottom.

A short left radical beside a long right radical.

A tall left radical beside a short right radical.

A narrow left radical beside a broad right radical.

A broad left radical beside a narrow right radical.

Leaving out strokes, merging strokes and substitution of radicals

Leaving out strokes.

Illustration by Wen Jingen

Substitution of some strokes.

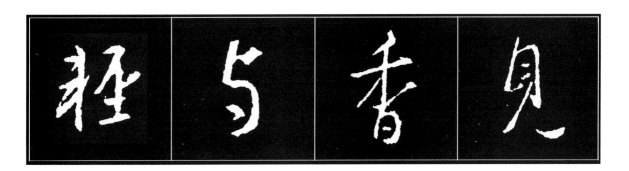

Illustration by Wen Jingen

Merging multiple strokes into a simpler shape.

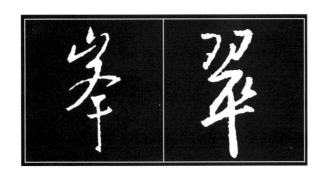

Illustration by Wen Jingen

Echoing and linking

Strokes may be linked physically or spiritually. In regular script calligraphy, strokes are often in a posture of joining to each other and thus making the whole character coherent. In running script calligraphy, strokes are often physically linked. But this device should not be used too much.

Physical linking

Compare the regular script:

Spiritual linking

In practising calligraphy, you must pay attention to the contrast between thick and slim strokes, long and short strokes, dense and sparse strokes, round and square strokes. Remember: practice makes perfect.

Here I recommend some masterpiece copybooks. Choose one to your taste and copy from it every day. In China such copybooks are available in all bookshops so you will have no difficulty in buying them.

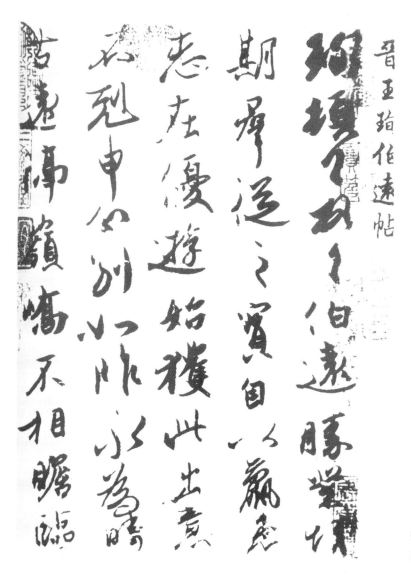

Calligraphy by Wang Xuan
(AD 350 — 401)

Stone inscription
by Li Yong (AD 678 — 747)

"Elegiac Address to his Nephew" by Yan Zhenqing
(AD 709 — 785)

Yan Zhenqing (AD 709-785) was noted for his sincerity and upright personality. He was an important general defending Pingyuan when An Lushan launched a rebellion against the central government. His brother and nephew were killed by the rebels. His full and robust regular script calligraphy has been regarded as a norm ever since his time. His running script and cursive script are excellent as well. His *Elegiac Address to his Nephew* 祭侄稿 has been praised as the second best running script piece in the world (the first one being Wang Xizhi's *Preface to the Poems at the Orchid Pavillion* 兰[蘭]亭序.

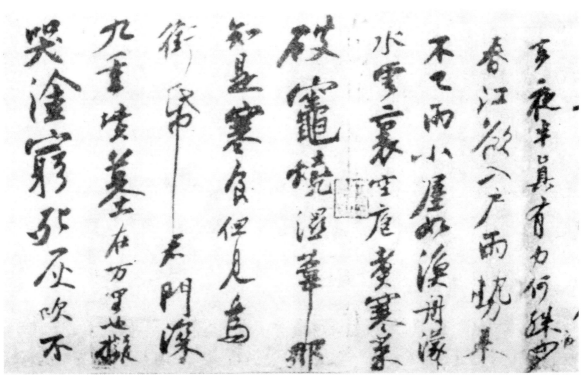

"Poem on Cold Food Day in Huangzhou" by Su Shi (1037 — 1101)

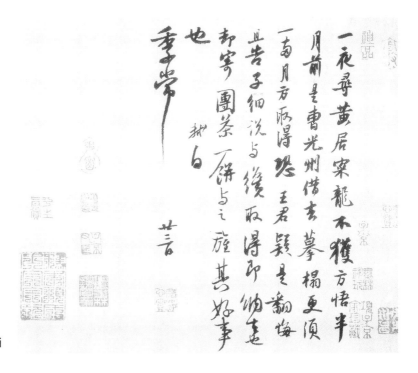

by Su Shi

Composition of Calligraphy: the Art of Black and White

To produce a masterpiece, good individual characters alone will not do, the calligrapher must ingeniously handle the relationship between characters and lines so as to make the whole piece a harmony of rhythmic diversities.

As a calligraphic work has two colours — black and white — the art of calligraphy is also called "the art of black and white". To compose a calligraphic work is to explore the relationship and arrangement of dots and strokes, the space between characters and lines, the size of characters, shades of ink, the bulkiness and slimness of strokes — all these give contrasts of black and white.

Here are few guidelines about composition for a beginner:

(1) Keep characters and lines in good order. In regular script calligraphy, all characters are arranged in vertical lines and horizontal rows. The space between characters is smaller than that between lines. Sometimes, the space between characters is rather large as well. In running script calligraphy, the space between characters is usually small and the space between lines is wide. Some calligraphers like Zheng Xie, make the lines intertwine — characters in one line often trespass on another line. In Zheng Xie's calligraphy, large and small characters alternate and swing to the left and the right, making the whole work full of variety and spontaneity.

From right to left or vice versa?

In ancient times Chinese people wrote from right to left in vertical lines. Even characters in a horizontal line read from right to left, contrary to the western convention. Nowadays, Chinese texts are printed the same way as in the west and Chinese people usually write horizontally from left to right. But Chinese calligraphers keep the old convention of writing from right to left in vertical lines. This, however, is not the rule. If you like, you may also try to create a calligraphic work by writing in horizontal left-right lines.

(2) Make a continuous whole. Arrange characters of different sizes, lengths, angles, bulkiness, directions and "postures" rationally so that the individual characters have continuity where everything is part of an integrated whole. The complete work should possess a momentum as if a kind of energy runs through the lines. Chinese calligraphers call this energy "air between lines" *hang qi* 行气[氣].

(3) Try to achieve variation. Different dots and strokes make the rhythm of the calligraphy. They can be compared to high and low pitches, strong and weak beats, quick and slow tempo in music. Therefore Chinese calligraphy is also called "soundless music". The rhythm in Chinese calligraphy manifests in the layout of a space with a changing density of black and white that is achieved by contrasts of square and round, straight and bending, broad and slim, straight and oblique, or vigorous and gentle strokes.

To achieve this, the calligrapher must pay attention to the speed of the movement of the brush and the strength he applies to the brush. To execute running script calligraphy, the movement of the brush should not be too fast or too slow. Too fast brushwork leads to sleek and weak strokes. On the other hand, sluggish brushwork tends to produce dull, ragged strokes.

(4) Add an inscription and seal imprints in proper places. After finishing your calligraphic work, you may add an inscription at the end of the main work. The inscription may indicate the dates and/or place of execution, your name, source of the content, and so on. Usually, the inscription should be written in smaller characters than the main body of your work. The inscription may be added at one side of the calligraphic work or two sides of it. Sometimes an inscription may contain the calligrapher's comment on something.

Calligraphy by Yang Ningshi (AD 873 — 954)

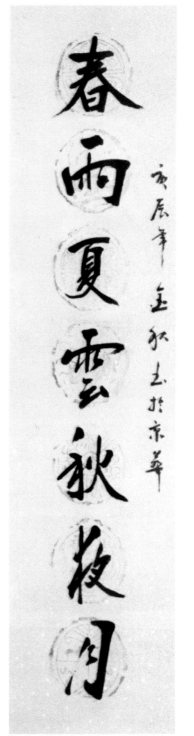

Text of the couplet reads: "Rain in spring, clouds in summer and the moon in autumn evening (right); Tang-dynasty poetry, Jin-dynasty calligraphy and Han-dynasty writing (left)" — These things are regarded as the most beautiful in the world.

One or more red seal imprints on a white paper with black characters will be particularly attractive to the eye. There are two kinds of seals used on art works: the seal of your name (*ming zhang* 名章) and the seal of a comment, a motto, a maxim or a verse (*xian zhang* 闲章 "leisure seal"). The legend of a seal is usually in the seal script (*zhuan shu* 篆书[書]).

seal
script

regular
script

person   large   water   sun   print

Seal and regular scripts, illustration
by Wen Jingen

"Taking reading as a pleasure"
— an impression of a "leisure
seal" (in red)

Formats of Backing and Framing

Chinese calligraphic works are usually backed and framed the same as for Chinese paintings.

Minimum backing

When Chinese characters are written in ink on unsized paper, the paper may become warped and the result is unsightly. Sophisticated backing and framing may involve many processes. You can do a minimum backing by yourself at home.

The minimum backing will make the paper bearing your work smooth and the ink shades distinct. Place your work face down, flat, on a clean table or glass surface and spray clean water onto the back of your calligraphy. Brush thin paste onto your work, lower another piece of unsized paper on top of it, brush out and leave to dry. When dry, remove it from the table or glass. To prevent the ink and colour on your paper from running when wet, you should wrap your work in newspaper, put it in a steamer and steam it for 20 minutes before you back it.

Formats

(1) Hand scroll *shou juan* 手卷. It is extremely long horizontally. Usually the viewer appreciates it whilst unrolling.

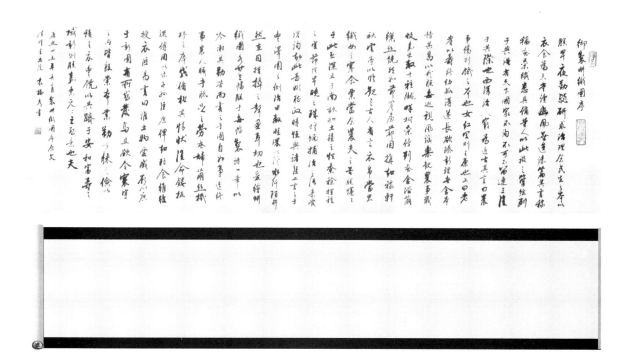

(2) Wide vertical scroll. *Zhong tang* 中堂 — literally, "centre of hall". It usually hangs at the centre of the wall in a saloon. It usually carries imposing and forceful characters. It may have only one character or many.

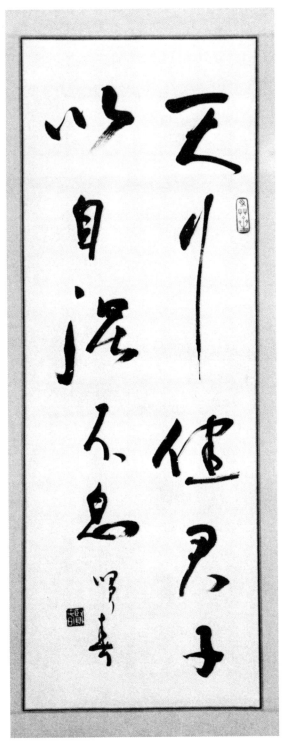

(3) Hanging scroll *tiao fu* 条[條]幅 — literally, tall narrow scroll. It may hang the same way as the *zhong tang*. Several (usually four or six) scrolls may hang side by side on the same wall. Chinese calligraphers often write a piece of prose or a poem on such scrolls. Try to make a good composition. Avoid writing a single character on the last line.

Fu Shan (1607-1684), an outstanding thinker, medical scientist, painter and calligrapher. Living during the interregnum of the Ming (1368-1644) and the Manchu Qing dynasties, he refused to cooperate with the conqueror Qing regime. His robust and forceful calligraphy has been praised for being imbued with his unyielding national integrity.

(4) Hanging couplet *duilian* 对联 [對聯]. Two antithetical lines are written on a couple of scrolls. The lines have the same number of characters. Over the Spring Festival (the New Year's Day according to the traditional Chinese calendar, or the "farmer's calendar") Chinese people, especially in rural areas, hang couplets on their doors. The couplet usually has one line on each scroll, but some large couplets may have many characters in several lines. Conventionally, the first line is on the right scroll.

Dragon-gate couplet *longmen dui* 龙门对[龍門對].

Each scroll has several lines of characters. The right scroll starts from the right and ends at the left, and the left one in the reverse order. The last line should be shorter than other lines. The whole couplet looks like a Chinese character "gate" *men* 門, hence the name (see p. 5).

(5) Horizontal scroll *hengfu* 横幅. It is shorter than a hand scroll and usually hangs in a frame on the wall facing the entrance in the saloon.

(6) Fan *shanmian* 扇面. There are two kinds of fans — the round fan and the folding fan. Suit the composition of your calligraphy to the format of the fan.

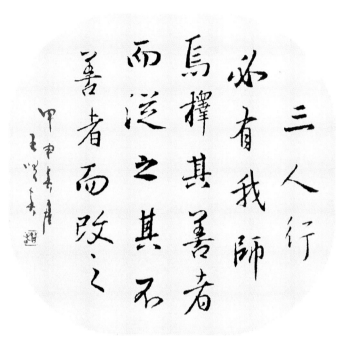

Fan with running script calligraphy of Wen Zhengming (1470 — 1559)

(7) Square sheet *doufang* 斗方. Such a sheet of paper is suitable to be framed and hung on the wall.

Creating Your Own Style

After a period of training, you will have a grounding of calligraphic techniques. Your next step is to initiate your own style. You cannot force yourself to be a copy of another calligrapher, because each person has his temperament and understanding of arts. Many great calligraphers start from copying from one copybook and then proceed to study more calligraphic masterpieces. By drawing on the merits of several masters and then deciding your preferences, a new personal style will emerge by and by.

Be inspired by things other than calligraphy.

Good artists often get inspiration from nature and everyday life. Zhang Xu was a master cursive script calligrapher. Gongsun Daniang was a good dancer. One day when Zhang Xu watched Gongsun dance with swords he got a sudden inspiration. He infused the movement of the sword dancer into his calligraphy and produced a masterpiece with dashing brushwork.

The calligrapher's emotion and frame of mind plays an important role too. The master calligrapher Yan Zhenqing produced his masterpiece *Elegiac Address to his Nephew* 祭侄稿 when he was grief-stricken by the death of his nephew (see p. 132).

Seek advice.

Hang your works on the wall and look at them from time to time. You may find defects in works which were at first quite satisfactory to you. Once you are unhappy with your old works, you will make a new step in your calligraphy creation. Experts' advice may open your eyes. There is a Chinese saying, "Hearing your remark I have learned more than I could from ten-year reading."

Cultivate your personality.

The style is the man. Moral and artistic cultivation plays an important part in your calligraphy.

A Glance at Chinese Calligraphy through the Dynasties

Chinese calligraphy dates back to no less than 3,700 years ago. Chinese calligraphy as an art discipline not only serves as a practical tool for recording Chinese people's thinking and historical events, but it has been appreciated for its abstract beauty. It is also a vehicle for cultivation of personality and means of ornamenting people's living quarters. Calligraphic works in scenic spots add attraction to the beautiful view. In China calligraphy is also an important item pursued by art collectors.

Scripts on bones, *jiaguwen* 甲骨文. During the Shang Dynasty (c. 1600 — c. 1100 BC) Chinese characters were carved on bones and tortoise shells, hence the name "shell-bone script" *jiaguwen*.

Later Chinese characters found their way onto bronze wares. Hence the name "metal script" *jinwen* 金文, or "bell and tripod script" *zhongdingwen* 钟[鐘]鼎文, nowadays known as "great seal script" *dazhuan* 大篆.

In BC 221 Qin Shi Huang (or Shi Huangdi of Qin), the First Emperor of the Qin Dynasty, unified China with armed forces and the Chinese writing system. This calligraphy is known as "small seal script" *xiaozhuan* 小篆, and is generally called "seal script" *zhuanshu* 篆书[書] today. It has been used in seal carving (hence the name), and is noted for the even lines and regular composition.

Seal script inscription on ancient stone

While seal script was in use, another script came into being. The new script has been called "official script" or "clerical script" *li shu* 隶书[隸書], because it was first used by officials or clerks in transcribing official documents. The official script was widely used during the Han Dynasty (206 BC — AD 220). Compared with the seal script, the official script became less pictographic. Round turning strokes in the seal script became square strokes in the official script. In addition the strokes were no longer of even width.

Since that time, the structure of the Chinese writing system has been stable and no great changes have taken place. On the other hand, the potential of the brushwork has brought forth new styles of calligraphy.

Cursive script *caoshu* 草书[書] is the result of rapid movement of the brush.

Huai Su (AD 725 — 785 or 737 — 799), a Buddhist monk and calligrapher, once a student of Yan Zhenqing, produced "wild cursive script" calligraphy.

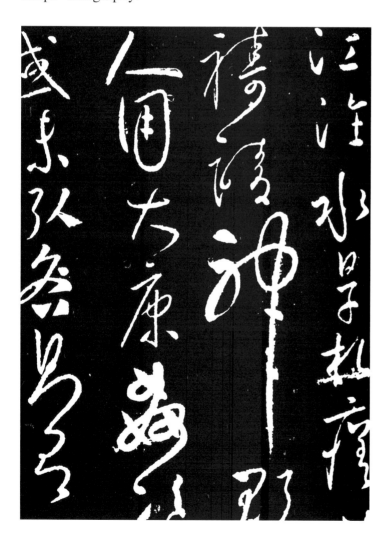

Cursive script by Huai Su

The regular script *kaishu* 楷书[書] came into being from the official script. Around the fourth century Zhong You and other calligraphers laid the foundation of this new style of calligraphy. Regular script has been the standard style ever since then.

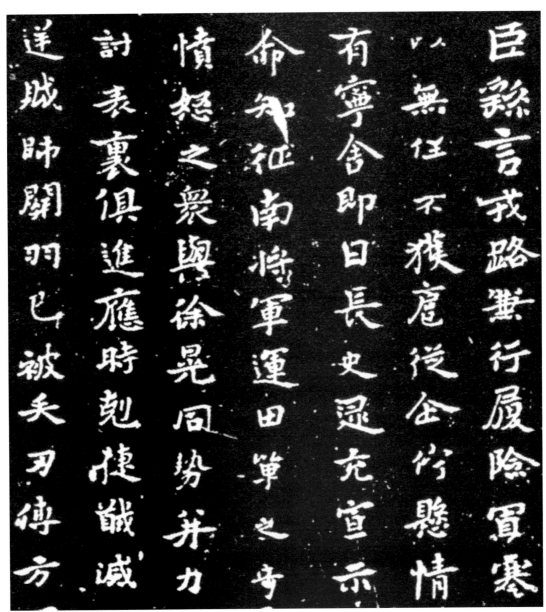

Early regular script calligraphy

Regular script calligraphy of the
8th — 9th centuries

The running script *xingshu* 行书[書], as featured in this book, is an intermediate form of the regular script and cursive script. It is easily executable and at the same time easily recognizable. It is a rather practical style and that is why running script calligraphy was widely used in correspondence and manuscripts.

Running script by Zhao Mengfu (1254 — 1322)

Wang Xizhi's *Preface to the Poems at the Orchid Pavillion* [*Lanting Xu* 兰[蘭]亭序] has been praised as the first masterpiece of running script calligraphy in the world. Unfortunately, the original of this masterpiece was entombed with the emperor Taizong (r. 627-648) of the Tang Dynasty who loved the masterpiece too dearly and ordered it be buried with him after his death. What we see today of the masterpiece are copies done by other calligraphers.

Su Shi (also known as Su Dongpo, 1037 — 1101) was a versatile writer and artist. The running script calligraphy of Su and his contemporaries breathed new air into Chinese calligraphy.

The Tang Dynasty (AD 618 — 907) saw the maturation of all styles of script, with the regular script and the cursive script having the most development.

From the 10th to the 14th century, running script became the main stream of Chinese calligraphy. Innovative calligraphers include Su Shi, Huang Tingjian, Mi Fu and others.

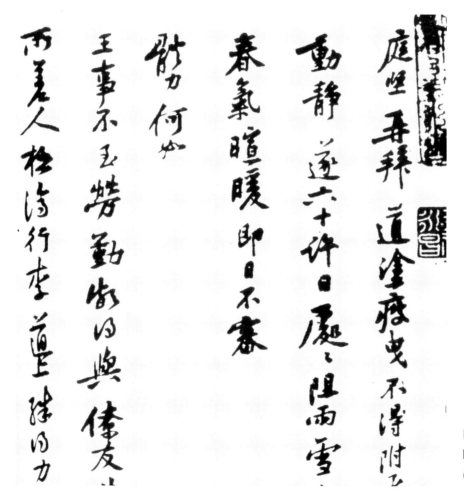

Running script
by Huang Tingjian
(1045 — 1105)

From the 15th century on, Chinese calligraphy has been further perfected with the emergence of calligraphers with distinct personal styles. The Qing Dynasty (1644 — 1911) saw the resurrection of seal script and official script calligraphy.

Running script by Wen Zhengming
(1470 — 1559)

Calligraphy, like other forms of art in the People's Republic of China (1949 —), is amazingly prosperous. This ancient art is embracing our contemporary world.

The poet Shen Yinmo (1883 — 1971) produced such excellent calligraphy that his reputation for calligraphy overshadowed his reputation in poetry creation.

Running Script by Lin Fan (b. 1931)

Traditional and simplified Chinese characters

In olden times, many Chinese characters had variation. Because Chinese characters are not easy to memorise, people tended to write the same characters in different ways. Some varieties are evidently simpler than the others. Efforts were made to unify the forms of Chinese writing with little success. In 1956 the government of the People's Republic of China announced a number of simplified characters as the norm. Since then simplified characters have been used in all publications. Traditional forms are also used, mainly in historical documents. Many calligraphers like to write the traditional characters because those are what they copy from ancient copybooks when they study calligraphy. But it is absolutely wrong to say traditional characters are more beautiful than the simplified ones.

Traditional	寫	進	見	雞	驢	歸	術	電	鄉
Simplified	写	进	见	鸡	驴	归	术	电	乡
Meaning	write	enter	see	chicken	donkey	return	skill	eletricity	village

图书在版编目（CIP）数据

怎样写行书 / 王贤春编著，温晋根编译.
－北京: 外文出版社, 2007
（怎样做系列）
ISBN 978-7-119-04860-4

I. 怎... II. ①王...②温... III. 行书—技法(美术) — 英文 IV. J292.113.5

中国版本图书馆 CIP 数据核字（2007）第 096752 号

责任编辑　温晋根
封面设计　蔡　荣
插图绘制　王贤春　温晋根
策　　划　王贤春　李振国　肖晓明　温晋根

外文出版社网址:
http://www.flp.com.cn
外文出版社电子信箱:
info@flp.com.cn
sales@flp.com.cn

怎样写行书

王贤春　著

*

© 外文出版社
外文出版社出版
（中国北京百万庄大街 24 号
邮政编码 100037)
北京雷杰印刷有限公司印刷
中国国际图书贸易总公司发行
（中国北京车公庄西路 35 号
北京邮政信箱第 399 号 邮政编码 100044)
2007 年(16 开)第 1 版
2007 年第 1 版第 1 次印刷
（英）
ISBN 978-7-119-04860-4
14000(平)
7-E-3760P